Office Song

A Play

Nick Warburton

A SAMUEL FRENCH ACTING EDITION

SAMUEL FRENCH

FOUNDED 1830

SAMUELFRENCH-LONDON.CO.UK
SAMUELFRENCH.COM

ISBN 978-0-573-12174-6

www.samuelfrench-london.co.uk

www.samuelfrench.com

FOR AMATEUR PRODUCTION ENQUIRIES

UNITED KINGDOM AND WORLD
EXCLUDING NORTH AMERICA
plays@SamuelFrench-London.co.uk
020 7255 4302/01

Each title is subject to availability from Samuel French,

depending upon country of performance.

The professional rights in this play are controlled by David Higham Associates Ltd, 7th Floor, Waverley House, 7–12 Noel Street, London W1F 8GQ.

OFFICE SONG

First performed by Stapleford Umbrella Drama Society
on 20th February 1997 at Stapleford, Cambridgeshire,
with the following cast:

Brian	Colin Lawrence
Claire	Jane Bower
Wendy	Sally Marsh

Director Peter Wood

Other plays by Nick Warburton published by Samuel French Ltd

Distracted Globe
Don't Blame It On The Boots
The Droitwich Discovery
Easy Stages
The Last Bread Pudding
The Loophole
Not Bobby
Receive This Light
Round the World with Class Six
Sour Grapes and Ashes
Zartan

OFFICE SONG

An office cloakroom

The room is dimly-lit and rather stark. It has coat-racks with coats and bags, a bin, and a few chairs stacked out of the way. A door at the back stands open

When the play begins, the throb of party music, a shaft of bright light, voices and bursts of laughter come through the door. It's the Christmas party at Cooper's; it's all going very well in there

Brian enters. He wears a suit with a cardigan under the jacket, and a party hat on his head. He stands in the light for a moment, looking back at the party. There is a particularly raucous burst of laughter and he shuts the door. He does not look happy. He comes forward, takes off his party hat, screws it up and tosses it in a bin. He begins to rummage through the coats. As he is doing this ——

The door opens again and Claire staggers in with a plastic beaker. She is giggling. Brian sees Claire and shrinks back among the coats, peering out

Claire (*shouting back through the door*) Get lost! No! I'm not doing it. (*She drinks; then, to herself*) I don't care who you are. I don't have to. So I'm not. (*She shuts the door and tosses the beaker in the bin. Then she whirls in a circle, snatching up a coat and dancing with it. She dances over to the light switch and puts the lights on*) Wow! (*To the coat*) Let's make the floor shake, you and me. Let's engage! (*She dances*) Do you come here often? Once a year? At Christmas? Me too. Sad, isn't it? Of course, I come here more than that really. Like every day of the bleeding year. Almost. Yeah, I know. It is. Really, really sad. You yearn for something to happen, don't you? I do. I'm always yearning, I am. Still, the party's warming up. Really? How kind of you to say so. You look pretty good to me, too. (*A fancy spin takes her close to the lurking Brian. She sees him peering through the coats, drops the coat she's dancing with and screams. It's a full-bodied scream and lasts several seconds. She tramples on the coat*)

Brian jumps out to calm Claire but doesn't know how. He dithers anxiously

Brian Don't — please, Claire ...

Claire turns and sees that it's only old Brian. The scream dies and she relaxes, still standing on the coat

Claire Oh. Brian.
Brian Look, I'm sorry... I was just...
Claire I thought it was one of the others. I thought ... well, for a moment there I thought you were going to ——
Brian Oh, good Lord, no. I came in for my coat ——
Claire Oh? Why?
Brian — only I couldn't find it. (*He nods at the coat Claire is standing on*) Till now.
Claire (*stepping off*) Oh. Right. You're not going, are you, Brian?
Brian (*picking up the coat*) I thought I would actually, yes.
Claire Oh, Brian, why? Just when it's picking up out there. They're about to do the talent spot, you know.
Brian Yes.
Claire You're all right, are you?
Brian (*putting the coat on*) Yes, yes. I just thought I'd ——
Claire Not got a headache or anything?
Brian Headache?
Claire Pretty dense sound in there.
Brian Oh, that. No, I ... well, it's not me, really.

Claire It could be, though. You should relax a little, you know. Let yourself go.

Brian That's what I am doing, actually.

Claire After all, it's only once a year.

Brian Thank goodness.

Claire What do you mean, that's what you are doing?

Brian Letting myself go.

She doesn't understand

Go home.

Claire You don't want to do that. (*She looks at him*) You could get yourself fixed up.

Brian Fixed up?

Claire All those girls in their party gear...

Brian Oh, no, I don't think so.

Claire Why not? They hardly know what they're doing in there, some of them.

Brian smiles wryly

(*Seeing his smile; hastily*) Not that they have to be sloshed or an ... (*As in "anything"*) I mean, I didn't mean ...

Brian It's all right, Claire. I've put in an appearance. That's all that was needed.

Claire You mean, you only came because you thought you had to? Who told you that?

Brian Camilla. Said I ought to show my face. Said it might be noticed if I didn't. By Mr Cooper.

Claire That doesn't make sense. How're they going to notice you if you're not there?

Brian Notice my absence, I suppose.

Claire Old Man Cooper? He's not noticing anything at the moment, believe me. He's had his head in Wendy's cleavage half the evening.

Brian Yes, well, there's that as well.

Claire That as well?

Brian Yes. You know.

Claire Oh. I see. Wendy.

Brian Well ...

Claire You mean it ought to be you?

Brian No. No, I... (*He changes the subject*) Anyway, you're not going, are you?

Claire Me? No, the night is but young, Brian. I only came in here because ... well, they're about to do the talent spot.

Brian Don't you like the talent spot?

Claire Oh, yes. It's a laugh. You know, people making prats of themselves. I think it's funny the way they spend all year worrying away at output figures and then kind of burst out and do impressions or something. They don't care. In fact, sometimes they don't even remember. No, it's a real laugh.

Brian Then why are you ...?

Claire I'm hiding. Eddie Mellor's trying to get me to take part.

Brian You?

Claire He says I should do the *Stripper*. You know, that music. He's got the tape. But I'm not having any of that.

Brian No, I don't blame you.

Claire So I'm keeping out of the way for a bit.

Brian Very sensible.

Claire It'll be all right once it's started. I won't be noticed then. I'll go out and have a look. But I'm not performing.

Brian Me neither.

Claire You could, though, Brian. Do a tap-dance or something.

Brian Good Lord, no.

Claire Or an impression. Know any impressions, do you?

Brian No. Well ...

Claire What?

Brian No.

Claire Go on.

Brian I have done a few impressions before, actually.

Claire Don't tell me. Frank Spencer.

Brian Who? Oh, no, I mean Dean Martin and stuff. You know, Doris Day.

Claire Doris Day? Doris Day? What, in drag?

Brian Certainly not. No, just the songs. I'm a bit of a fan, see. Wonderful melodies they had in those days. Of course, I'd never dream of doing it in public.

Claire Why not?

Brian It's just an interest, really. Very private. In fact, forget I said it … you won't mention it to anyone else, will you? You know what they're like round here, some of them.

Claire Your secret is safe with me. Doris.

Brian I'm not really at ease with gatherings, see. Never have been. In fact, Mum was only saying this morning, about parties, you know.

Claire What about them?

Brian How I never liked them. Even as a kiddie. She was reminding me of this party I went to when I was about eight. Everyone skipping about and stuffing jelly. The boys with little ties on and the girls in those puffed out dresses. And me kind of —not joining in.

Claire Ah, shame!

Brian I felt this great urge to join in, but a great fear as well. Stupid, really. She said when she came to fetch me I was practically rigid.

Claire Must've been all those girls in their dresses.

Brian How do you mean?

Claire Never mind.

Brian No, I was kind of rigid with embarrassment. So Mum said. Well, it's not everyone's cup of tea, is it?

Claire So I can't persuade you to give us your Doris Day?

Brian I don't think so.

Claire It can't be as bad as Mr Williams doing *Just a Song at Twilight*. Or Sharon's disco routine.

Brian Sharon?

Claire From Accounts. You must've seen it. She's very uninhibited.

Brian I've never stayed long enough for the talent spot, actually.

Claire Really? I haven't noticed. I mean, I haven't noticed you not being there.

Brian Good.

Claire You ought to give it a try, though, Brian. Watching it, I mean. Mr Cooper does this monologue thing. He wins, of course. He says he's not going to do anything but he always does. They all start chanting: yes, yes, yes! And he pretends he doesn't want to but in the end he does. This sort of spoken thing about brown boots.

Brian Brown boots?

Claire Somebody wears these brown boots to a funeral or something. It's kind of sad. Then we all clap and he wins. I mean, we're all bum-lickers at heart, aren't we?

Brian Are we?

Claire Oh, yes. After all, they prefer Sharon. Her bra came off last year.

Brian Really? How dreadful.

Claire Sort of accidentally on purpose. It went a storm. But Old Man Cooper still won.

Brian I suppose you're right. I suppose that's why I'm here now.

Claire In case Sharon loses her bra again?

Brian No, I mean being here though not being a party animal as such. To keep the right side of Mr Cooper. Like you said.

Claire Oh, yeah. Bum-lickers all. It's the human condition, Brian. You haven't seen my bag, have you?

Brian I don't know. What's it look like?

Claire Small, blue with a long strap.

Brian goes back to look for the bag

(*Dancing again*) It's got my ciggies in it. Unless you've got ciggies, have you, Brian?

Brian No, no. I don't ...

The door flies open and Wendy bursts in with a sheet of paper

Wendy (*shouting back through the door*) You bloody animal! They've got gadgets for animals like you, you know! (*She slams the door*) That'd stop you in your tracks.

Claire Wendy! Join the party! The off-party party.
Wendy Manoeuvred me into the photocopying room. Animal.
Claire Who?
Wendy Who'd you think? Said he had something to show me. You know what it was?
Claire What?

Wendy hands her the sheet of paper

(*Studying the paper but unable to understand it*) What is it?
Wendy I told you. He got me into the photocopying room.
Claire So?
Wendy Can't you see it?

They stare at the paper. Brian comes up behind them with Claire's bag

Brian Is this it?

Wendy jumps and screams

Claire Calm down, calm down. It's only Brian.
Wendy God! Where did he spring from?
Brian Sorry …
Claire He's just on his way home.
Wendy Creeping about like Jack the bloody Ripper ...
Brian Sorry. I thought you saw me...
Claire It's only Brian. Brian the Ripper.
Wendy Couldn't you've coughed or something?
Brian Sorry …
Claire It's all right. You're quite safe. Here, Brian, what do you make of this?
Wendy Don't show him.
Claire Oh, go on. What do you reckon it is?
Brian I don't know. It's a bit grainy ...
Claire Give us a clue.

Wendy Well ... if Old Man Cooper was to come in here now, he'd
  bring one with him.
Claire Sorry. No idea.
Wendy Come on. Brian's got one. Probably.

Claire suddenly sees what it is. Her jaw drops

Claire My God!
Wendy See?
Claire God, it's obvious now, isn't it? Sticks out like a sore thumb.
  But why'd you say Old Man Cooper would bring one in? That's
  what threw me.
Wendy Well, he would, wouldn't he? Obviously.
Claire The way you said it, though, I thought you meant tucked
  under his arm or something.
Wendy Erugh! Gross!
Brian You mean it's — it's ...
Wendy Exactly, Brian. I thought you'd've got it straight off. I
  mean, you start with an advantage over Claire and me.
  Presumably.
Brian But this is disgusting, Wendy.
Claire Who is it?
Wendy Well, I assume it's Eddie. He gave it to me.
Claire Eddie Mellor?
Wendy Bloody animal.
Brian I can hardly believe it. He's not normally like this.
Claire Oh, he is, Brian.
Brian I suppose he just wasn't thinking...
Claire Yes he was, Brian.
Brian I mean, it's so disrespectful. Someone ought to tell him.
Wendy I told him.
Brian He probably didn't realize. Maybe I should have a word with
  him ...
Wendy (*after a long look at Brian*) You?
Brian Well, I think someone ought to.
Wendy Yes, you're right. Go on, then.

Claire I shouldn't bother, Brian. I don't think he'd appreciate it.

Brian But he has to know. He probably thinks it's just a laugh ——

Claire It is a bit.

Brian — but he's shocked Wendy. He ought to realize that. (*He edges to the door*) I'll have a word, if you like.

Claire No, Brian.

Wendy Let him go, why not?

Brian (*hesitating by the door*) The thing is, he might do it again if someone doesn't point it out to him.

Wendy Of course he will.

Brian hovers by the door and the women stare at him

Brian Right. So.

Claire I should take a drink or two when you get in there, if I was you.

Brian smiles faintly and exits

You shouldn't've let him. Eddie'll kill him

Wendy Me? I couldn't stop him, could I?

They study the photocopy at arms' length for a while

Claire I've never seen anything like it.

Wendy Oh, yes?

Claire Not under glass, I haven't.

Wendy It's like a goblin with its face pressed up against a window, isn't it?

They continue studying the photocopy

Claire I'll tell you something.

Wendy What?

Claire He's used the enlarging facility.

Wendy Do you reckon?
Claire Absolutely. Actually, now I come to think about it, you can tell it's Eddie.
Wendy How?
Claire I don't know. It's the eyes, I think.
Wendy Believe me, Claire, these are not eyes.
Claire No, I mean the look in his eyes. The way he looks at you. Kind of pervy. He tried to get me to do the *Stripper*.
Wendy No!
Claire Yes. That's why I'm in here.
Wendy To get yourself psyched up?
Claire To keep out of his way.
Wendy Somebody needs to get in his bloody way. He needs sorting out.
Claire Someone is. Right now.
Wendy I don't think Brian Budd's going to get very far. (*She looks at the photocopy*) It must be Mellor. It's got that middle management look about it
Claire Sort of perky and eager.
Wendy And not particularly executive.
Claire Executive?
Wendy Yes. I mean, it's obviously not Old Man Cooper, is it?
Claire No, I see what you mean. It lacks the personality. Whatever else you say about Old Man Cooper, he's got personality. Compared to most blokes round here.
Wendy Compared to most blokes round here, my desk's got personality. And it's more interesting to talk to.

Wendy screws up the paper and lobs it in the bin

Claire Oooh. Painful.
Wendy Let's hope.
Claire There's always Brian, you know.
Wendy Brian?
Claire To talk to.
Wendy You must be joking.

Claire I don't know. It was kind of gallant of him, to go in there and face up to Eddie.

Wendy He's not facing up to him, he's having a word with him. Which, let's face it, is pathetic.

Claire He obviously likes you.

Wendy Come to that, Claire, who doesn't?

Claire No, really likes you. He seemed quite upset when I told him about Old Man Cooper having his ... you know, having his ...

Wendy His what?

Claire Being all over you.

Wendy God. Brian? Brian Budd. (*She looks at the door*) I do hope not. I sincerely hope not.

Claire Why?

Wendy Because it's an appalling thought, Claire, that's why. It turns my stomach to think of it.

Claire finds a chair and sits. She lights up a cigarette

Claire He's not that bad, Wendy.

Wendy It pisses me off, Claire, it really does. Bloody men. They treat you like —like flesh.

Claire Well, you are flesh, aren't you? Anyway, with Brian it's probably just a spiritual thing.

Wendy Spiritual? Don't be fooled by him, Claire. Just because he looks like Postman Pat on sedatives.

Claire Oh, poor old Brian.

Wendy They're all the same. It's all flesh with them. Anyway, he eats with his mouth open.

Claire What's wrong with that?

Wendy You sit near him in the canteen and you'll find out. A constant spray of cheese and pickle. Like eating next to a muck-spreader.

Claire (*laughing*) No, don't.

Brian trails in. Wendy and Claire stare at him

Wendy Well?

Brian I couldn't find him, actually.

Wendy Couldn't find him?

Brian Well, he was deep in conversation ...

Claire He hasn't got any conversation.

Brian Well, you know ...

Wendy So you didn't like to interrupt and he gets away with it. Thank you very much. (*She moves away and turns her back*)

Brian Sorry. It didn't seem like a good time. It might be better to talk to him in the work environment.

Wendy Oh, yes. Of course. I can live with the humiliation till then, I'm sure.

Brian Look, I think I'd better be on my way.

Wendy (*turning back*) On your way?

Brian Probably.

Wendy Before the talent spot?

Claire Definitely before the talent spot.

Wendy Oh, Mr Budd, you disappoint me. You're not offering anything, then?

Brian I don't think so. I'd rather just go ...

Wendy You want us to hide you?

Brian What? No, why should I want that?

Wendy If Eddie's on the rampage. You can cower behind us.

Brian It's not a case of cowering, actually.

Wendy Come over here, then. Talk to us. We won't bite you, Brian.

Brian (*coming forward*) Talk about what?

Wendy I don't know. Talent. What are you planning to do?

Brian I'm not planning to do anything.

Wendy But you must have some sort of talent hidden behind that cardigan, Brian.

Brian Not really.

Wendy (*to Claire*) Honestly, who wears a cardigan to a Christmas party? (*She sets a chair for Brian*) You're a bit of a mystery round here, did you know that? No-one knows anything about you. Sit down a moment.

Brian sits nervously

You can't come to the Christmas party and then just slink away again. I mean, what's the point of coming at all?

Brian I didn't want to come at all.

Claire No, Old Man Cooper issued instructions apparently.

Wendy Really? What, 'I must have that Brian Budd at my party. It just won't go otherwise.'

Brian Not exactly.

Claire He has to be seen around. Cooper told Camilla and Camilla told Brian.

Brian Just to join in with things a bit, you know.

Wendy Well, you're not doing that, are you? Not by sloping off. That way we get no nearer to the mystery at all.

Claire What mystery?

Wendy The mystery that is Brian Budd. What makes him tick. You do tick, do you, Brian?

Brian How d'you mean 'tick'?

Wendy What brings you to life?

Claire You do, Wendy.

Brian What?

Wendy Now then, Claire. You're embarrassing us. Let's keep smut off the agenda, shall we? Let's just concentrate on the business in hand.

Claire And what's that?

Wendy What Brian here is going to do for the talent spot. That's what you'd prefer, isn't it, Brian?

Brian Yes. I mean, no ...

Wendy You don't want Claire delving into your private life ...

Brian No, I don't.

Wendy Your fantasies.

Brian Of course not.

Wendy Quite right. Nor do I. Not your fantasies, anyway. So you'd prefer to concentrate on the talent spot ...

Brian I didn't say that.

Wendy What are you going to give us?

Brian Sorry? I mean, I'm not quite with you ...

Wendy There must be something, for God's sake. Unless — unless you're one of these sad types who have no talent at all. Are you?

Brian Probably.

Wendy That's a pity, because talent leads to talent, you know.

Claire How'd you work that out?

Wendy *The* talent. Sharon and friends. Sharon likes a man who's prepared to flaunt it. (*To Claire*) Hey, look at this. He's shaking with emotion.

Brian No I'm not ...

Wendy I do believe he's about to fly off the handle.

Claire Don't, Wendy.

Wendy What?

Claire You're winding him up.

Brian No, it's all right. It takes a lot to wind me up, actually.

Wendy Ooh, a challenge.

Brian It's just that there's nothing I can do.

Wendy That can't be true. Come on, Mr Budd. We're panting with anticipation here. (*Beat*) Nothing.

Brian Look, there really is nothing, believe me.

Wendy You're very defiant when you're worked up, you know. What do you do for fun? In the evenings?

Brian What?

Wendy You haven't got a train set, have you?

Brian No.

Wendy That's good, because they want something with a bit of kick to it. So what do you do?

Brian Well ...

Wendy Yes?

Brian I don't know.

Claire Oh, Brian, that is so sad.

Brian I mean, I have to think.

Wendy Shall I tell you what I do? I feed the cat. I rinse the Whiskas tin. I wash my hair.

Claire That's not what I've heard.

Wendy Sometimes the excitement is so fierce I have to lie down and do deep breathing. It's a very sensual thing, hair-washing.

Claire Can't say I've noticed.

Wendy It is if the alternative's washing out Whiskas tins. And you can walk around tossing your hair, like they do on the ads.

Claire It's not natural, that. It makes you dizzy.

Wendy I like being dizzy. It gets my blood thrumming.

Brian Gets it what?

Wendy Thrumming. Tingling. Only, hair-washing's not generally accepted as party entertainment. So I'm no good, am I? And Claire's no good either. I mean, look at her. I don't think she's going to wring much applause from that lot out there. Which just leaves you, Mr Budd.

Claire I know: tell her about the singing, Brian.

Wendy What?

Brian Claire. You said ——

Claire He likes to sing.

Brian You said you wouldn't say about that.

Claire Did I? Sorry.

Wendy He likes to sing. Well, well, well. All on your own?

Claire Yeah. In his bath, probably.

Brian No, not always. Sometimes I go to this group ——

Claire And they all sit in their baths and sing!

Brian No ...

Wendy But that's wonderful. Brian the Singer. What do you sing?

Brian The group does folk songs and stuff. A bit of Country and Western. But I prefer ... (*He stops*)

Wendy What? Don't stop there.

Brian No. I don't want to ... I don't have to ...

Claire Doris Day!

Brian Claire!

Claire Ooops.

Wendy Never! Doris Day? You're kidding.

Brian There's nothing wrong with Doris Day. She had real sparkle, she did.

Wendy Which is why you took to her, obviously. Well, I think we've found the key.

Claire It's cabaret time, Brian. You want to get out there and knock 'em dead.

Brian I blinking don't.

Wendy Brian Budd and the Buddies!

Claire The Cotton-buds!

Wendy Yes! But we can't send him out like that, can we?

Brian I'm not going out there ...

Wendy No, we're not heartless, are we?

Claire Only a bit.

Wendy No. We ought to audition him. See if he's up to it.

Claire Yeah!

Wendy So. Why don't you sing for us, Brian? Now?

Brian What?

Claire Oh go on. For Wendy's sake.

Wendy For my sake? Oh, Claire, do you mean to say he'd sing for me? Would you do that, Brian?

Brian I'm not sure it's your cup of tea, actually.

Wendy Why? Is it rude?

Brian Of course not.

Wendy I didn't know old Doris went in for rude songs.

Brian You should never have mentioned this, Claire. I did say.

Claire Oh, don't make such a fuss about it.

Wendy And you can't creep back into your shell now. You should've thought about that before you started sounding off about this wonderful voice of yours.

Brian I didn't. I never said it was any good ...

Wendy We'll be the judge of that, won't we, Claire? Come on, then. Give us a song.

Brian Well ...

Wendy Sing, Brian! Sing!

Brian clears his throat and sings a verse of "Secret Love" quietly and apologetically. When he has finished, he pauses, hanging his head, humiliated and sweating with shame

Was that it? I mean, was that it?

Claire Very nice, Brian.

Wendy Nice? It was pathetic. And you do that for fun, do you? Because it didn't sound like fun to me.

Claire I don't know. He's got a nice little voice.
Wendy It was little all right. Like a mouse.
Brian I normally sing in the group, see.
Wendy Normally, do you?
Brian Yes.
Claire In the group, in the bath.
Brian No.
Wendy (*nodding at the door*) Well, you're not going to get your group in there, are you? Let alone their baths. And, anyway, it was so half-hearted.
Brian In fact, I didn't really want to ——
Wendy Things don't happen if you don't make them, Brian. Sit on your arse and shuffle papers for Cooper's all your life and that's what you'll end up with: shuffled papers. Do it again.
Brian Oh, no, I don't think ——
Wendy Let your hair down a bit. And big, Brian. Make it big!
Brian This is blinking ridiculous.
Claire Now, now, don't get ratty.
Wendy Just sing.

Brian is suddenly resigned. He takes a breath to sing but Wendy stops him

And take your coat off. And that cardigan.
Brian What?
Wendy You can't sing in that. You look like some old uncle.

Brian takes his coat off. He pulls his cardigan off and flings it aside

Brian (*singing*) Once I had a secret ——
Wendy Bigger.
Brian (*singing louder*) Once I had a ——
Wendy (*stopping Brian*) Just a minute, just a minute. He needs a platform, a stage.
Claire Maybe he should stand on the chair.
Wendy Yes. Stand on the chair, Brian.

Brian stands on the chair

(*Walking round Brian, pondering*) Yes. Better. OK, then. Take it
away.

Brian sings the verse again, Wendy conducting and calling out as
he sings

Wendy That's more like it. Keep it up, Brian!

The song comes to an end

   Yes! That was fun, wasn't it?
Brian Well ...
Wendy I could tell it was. Couldn't you, Claire?
Claire Well ...
Wendy He was beginning to have fun.
Claire He looks a bit uncomfortable to me.
Brian That's because I am.
Wendy Take your tie off, then. Loosen up.

Brian hesitates

   Go on.

Brian removes his tie

   Undo your shirt.
Brian No ...
Claire Yeah! Undo the buttons, Brian.
Brian I don't see how it's necessary to undo ——
Wendy It's a sexy number, Brian, and you're buttoned up. Tense.
Brian I don't mean to be.
Claire You can't give it everything if you're tense, can you?
Brian Probably not.
Wendy If you give it everything you've got, you'll have women
   throwing their knickers at you.
Brian I don't want women throwing their knickers at me.
Wendy Yes you do. But you've got to persuade them. (*To Claire*)
   You're not going to throw your knickers at him looking like that,
   are you?

Claire Absolutely not.
Wendy See? So undo the buttons, Brian.
Brian (*in an attempt to be firm*) Look, I'm sorry, Wendy, but I think
  this ——
Wendy Let's see his chest, Claire.
Brian No, please ——
Wendy Why not? What's to be ashamed of.
Brian Nothing, but.
Wendy You've got pierced nipples or something?
Brian Of course not.
Wendy No. So you undo the buttons, Claire.
Claire (*hesitating a little*) I'm not sure he wants ——
Wendy Don't spoil it now. Lend the man a hand. (*Beat*) He'd like
  that; I can tell. He's not saying but it's what he wants. He just
  needs a bit of enccuragement.
Brian I can't see how taking your shirt off ——
Claire (*beginning to undo Brian's buttons*) You will see, Brian. It'll
  release something in you.
Wendy Of course it will. The waft of Old Spice. A sense of danger.
  The true animal that is Brian Budd.

Brian hangs his head and allows Claire to proceed

Claire He's a bit sweaty.
Brian Well of course I blooming am.
Wendy Now then. Don't get snappy. We're putting ourselves out
  for you, you know. Right. A deep breath. And again!
Brian (*singing*) Once I had a secret love ——
Wendy What?
Brian (*speaking*) Once I had a secret love.
Wendy Exactly, Brian. *Love.* Passion. This is a man in love, and
  that's just not coming through at the moment.
Claire Maybe he should curl his lip a bit.
Wendy Yes. Try it.

Brian curls his lip. Claire laughs

Claire Oo-er. The milk's off.

Wendy Love, Brian, love. You're a man who's bottled up his passion for too long.
Brian That's as maybe ...
Wendy Your mind is seething with passion. Memories of illicit nights. Twisted sheets and perfumed air. What are you thinking about?
Brian Camilla.
Claire (*shocked*) Camilla?
Brian I mean I'm thinking what happens if she blinking well walks in right now.
Wendy Life is nothing without risk, Brian. Come down here a moment.

Brian climbs down from the chair

Close your eyes.

Brian closes his eyes nervously. Wendy puts her hand under his shirt. He opens his eyes

Close them! Now what are you thinking about?
Brian (*tensely*) Nothing.
Wendy Remember last night, Brian?
Brian No.
Wendy Yes you do. Last night. You and me. Two whisky glasses by the bed. What we said. And what we did.
Claire Oo-er.
Wendy Remember?
Brian Sort of ...
Claire This is news to me.
Wendy Shut up, Claire. It's coming back to you, isn't it, Brian?
Brian Yes. It's coming back ...
Wendy You've had some bad thoughts.
Brian Yes.
Wendy And you're a bad man, aren't you?
Brian Yes, I am, actually.
Wendy Bad-arsed Brian.

Brian (*opening his eyes*) Yes!
Wendy And you sing... (*she kisses him lightly*) ... a bad-arsed song.
Brian Yes. Yes, I do.
Wendy (*abruptly breaking away*) So sing.

Brian climbs back on the chair, wild-eyed

Claire (*To Wendy*) What was all that about?
Wendy A bit of harmless fantasy, that's all.
Claire I thought his eyes were going to pop right out.
Wendy They might yet. (*To Brian*) OK, Brian?
Brian Yes.
Wendy Then take it away!

Brian sings the song again, this time with passion and vigour. It's not necessarily good, but it is vital, and unlike anything he's shown before

The Lights change as he sings

During the song, Brian jumps from the chair and dances with abandon, tossing coats from their pegs et cetera. He sees Claire and heads for her. Claire backs off, appalled, and hides among the coats. Brian turns to Wendy, spins her around and then kisses her. Wendy is shocked and slaps him hard

The Lights suddenly return us to cold reality. The song ends abruptly, unfinished. There is a devastating silence. Brian looks at Wendy, trying to work out what's just happened. She slaps him again. Slowly Brian begins to sob. He falls to his knees and curls up among the coats. Wendy backs away from him

Claire (*emerging from hiding*) What did you do that for?

Wendy turns away and does not answer

Brian? Brian? Are you all right?

Brian Leave me alone.
Claire (*to Wendy*) Now look.
Wendy What?
Claire Can't you see what you've done?
Wendy Me? I haven't done anything.

Wendy turns back to Brian and pulls him to his knees

Pull yourself together, Brian.
Brian Don't … please ...
Wendy You did it, didn't you?
Brian Look, I'm sorry ... I didn't mean ...
Wendy Don't be stupid.
Brian I don't know what happened ...
Claire I can tell you what happened ...
Brian For a moment I was ... I mean, I'm sorry if I ——
Wendy There's nothing to be sorry about. It was a bit of fun, that's
  all.
Claire What's the matter with you? Can't you see what you've
  done?
Wendy I told you before. I haven't done anything. I haven't done
  anything, have I, Brian?
Brian No, no. Of course not ...
Wendy See? (*To Brian*) You did what you wanted to do, didn't
  you?
Claire He did what you made him do.
Wendy Stop snuffling, Brian.

Wendy kneels behind Brian and he controls himself a little

What are people going to think? They come in here and find you
  snuffling ...
Claire Leave him alone.
Wendy A bit late for that now, Claire.
Claire He's a bloody wreck ...
Wendy And what do you intend to do about it? See him home? Hold
  his hand to the bus stop? You hear this, Brian? Claire thinks

you're a wreck. That's not very nice of her, is it? (*She kisses the top of Brian's head*) You and me, we know different.
Claire God, you're sick.
Wendy (*gesturing*) Go ahead then. Help him. Sister Claire to the rescue.
Claire I'm not going near him. I mean, look at him.
Wendy He looks all right to me.
Claire I've a good mind to tell someone.
Wendy Tell them what, Claire?
Brian No, don't. Please, Claire. I'm all right, really. I'm all right …
Claire You're not all right, Brian. You bloody flipped just then. God knows what you might've gone on to.
Brian Honestly, Claire. I mean, you know me.
Claire I thought I knew you.

Brian turns to look at Claire. He makes as if to get up

(*Backing away*) Don't come near me! You ought to be put away, the pair of you.
Brian Claire!

Claire rushes out

(*Trying to get up*) Claire!

Wendy puts her arms round Brian and holds him

Wendy Let her go. (*She strokes his hair*) She's not going to tell anyone. I mean, she can't, can she?
Brian Can't she?
Wendy I don't think she really understood. You understand, though, Brian, don't you?
Brian Do I? (*Beat*) All the same, I hope she won't.
Wendy Don't worry about it. Anyway, what can she say?

Brian turns to Wendy. They kneel among the coats facing each other like birds in a nest

Brian Look, Wendy, about that ... I mean, just now ...

Wendy Forget it.

Brian It wasn't ... I didn't mean to ...

Wendy What?

Brian I don't know. I'm sorry, that's all.

Wendy You mustn't be. Don't be sorry any more. (*She gets up and moves away*) It's what pisses me off about you, actually.

Brian What, being sorry?

Wendy All the bloody time. You put your head round the door on a Monday morning and I see it stamped on your face. Sorry. Sorry. Take a break for a moment, will you? Give it a rest.

Brian I don't know; putting my head round the door, after the holiday — I mean, I don't know how I'm going to face it ...

Wendy (*wandering over to the bin and taking out the photocopy which she uncrumples as she speaks*) Oh, Brian, what difference is it going to make?

Brian But I can't pretend it hasn't happened, can I?

Wendy Why should you? Anyway, what did happen? You sang a song for us ...

Brian I lost control ...

Wendy Yes, well, control wasn't doing you a lot of good from where I was standing.

Brian But you don't do that, do you? You don't just ... (*He holds his head in his hands and can't go on. He begins to sob a little*)

Wendy watches Brian a moment, then smooths out the photocopy and places it so he'll see it. She kneels beside him and cradles him in her arms, rocking him to silence

Wendy It's all right ... it's all right, Brian ... It really, really doesn't matter.

Brian (*seeing the photocopy*) Is that ...?

Wendy Yes.

Brian I nearly spoke to him, you know. He was talking to Sharon, kind of leaning into her with his arm propped on the wall ... The music ...

Wendy I know, Brian. It doesn't matter.

Brian It does, though. I stood behind him, a couple of steps from his back, and the words were in my head all right. 'Mellor. I want a word with you, Mellor.' But I couldn't say them. I backed off. (*Beat*) I should've ... I should've done something.

Wendy It's not worth it.

Brian It is. I mean ... (*He pauses*) You are.

Wendy picks up the photocopy and offers it to Brian

Wendy Tell you what, then, Brian: why don't you tear it up for me?

Brian Tear it up?

Wendy If it makes you feel better.

Brian All right. All right, I will. (*He slowly tears the photocopy into strips*)

Wendy There you are. It's a start, isn't it?

Brian Yes.

Wendy You feel better?

Brian A bit. Because he had no right ... I mean what he did was ... I mean, it was worse than me.

Wendy It was, but you have to take things in stages, Brian. You go out there now and try to sort him out, what'll happen?

Brian I don't know.

Wendy He won't like it and he won't put up with it.

Brian He'll turn nasty.

Wendy He already is nasty. But we don't want you getting pulped, do we? That's not going to get us anywhere.

Brian No.

Wendy So we do it in stages. We give it some thought.

Brian Plan, you mean?

Wendy Plan. Exactly.

Brian Follow him home — come up behind him——

Wendy Maybe, yes.

Brian Smash his blinking head in.

Wendy Why not? We're adults, aren't we? We can come up with something? You and me. (*Beat*) The photocopy was by no means the least of his crimes, you know.

Brian What do you mean?
Wendy It was the tip of a very murky iceberg.
Brian No. What did he ...?
Wendy I don't want to go into details. I will just say, he made me very unhappy.
Brian You should've told me.
Wendy Why? Would you've done anything about it?
Brian (*Beat*) No. No, I don't suppose so.
Wendy Not then, you wouldn't. Maybe it's different now.
Brian Yes. You're right, Wendy. It is different now.
Wendy Given time — and planning.
Brian I could do something ...
Wendy And a new strength of purpose. We'll talk about it, Brian. We'll think of something, I'm sure we will.

Wendy cradles Brian and rocks him

The Lights fade to Black-out

FURNITURE AND PROPERTY LIST

On stage: Coat racks with coats and bags
Claire's handbag containing cigarettes and lighter
Stacked chairs
Bin

Off stage: Plastic beaker (**Claire**)
Sheet of paper (**Wendy**)

LIGHTING PLOT

Practical fittings required: nil
Interior. The same throughout

To open:	Dim light on cloakroom with bright light through door

Cue 1   **Claire** switches on the lights   (Page 1)
Bring up cloakroom lights

Cue 2   **Brian** sings   (Page 21)
Lights change

Cue 3   **Wendy** slaps **Brian**   (Page 21)
Lights return to normal setting

Cue 4   **Wendy** cradles **Brian** and rocks him   (Page 26)
Black-out

EFFECTS PLOT

Cue 1   As play begins   (Page 1)
Throb of party music from behind door;
continue throughout play

9 780573 121746

Breakfast for One

A comedy

David Foxton

Samuel French—London
New York-Toronto-Hollywood

FOR AMATEUR PRODUCTION ENQUIRIES

**UNITED KINGDOM AND WORLD
EXCLUDING NORTH AMERICA**
plays@SamuelFrench-London.co.uk
020 7255 4302/01

Each title is subject to availability from Samuel French,

depending upon country of performance.

BREAKFAST FOR ONE

First performed by Dewsbury Arts Group at their Studio
Theatre in February 2001 with the following cast:

Marcel Morisot	David Rogers
Honorine	Alison Rust
Yvette Signac	Sally-Ann Burley
Claude Vallette	Gary Clayton
Vincent Signac	Andrew Madden

Directed by David Wood

CHARACTERS

Marcel Morisot, a personable young man
Honorine, a maid
Yvette Signac
Claude Vallette, a vagrant
Vincent Signac, a lawyer, husband to Yvette

The action of the play takes place in the apartment of Monsieur and Madame Signac in Paris. Not-too-early morning

Time — 1895

Other plays by David Foxton published by Samuel French Ltd

Card Play
Caught on the Hop
The Crowns, the King and the Long Lost Smile
Perkin and the Pastrycook
Rabbit
The Real Story of Puss in Boots

BREAKFAST FOR ONE

The elegant hall/dining-room area of the Paris apartment of Monsieur and Madame Signac. The end of the nineteenth century. Early morning; but not too early

Among the usual dining-room furniture is a screen large enough for a person to hide behind. On the table, breakfast is set for one

When the play begins, a man, Marcel Morisot, enters rather furtively from the direction of the front door of the apartment, L. *He peers around rather apprehensively*

Marcel (*in a stage whisper*) Marie-Céleste! … Marie-Céleste! (*He looks around and, indeed, moves around, carefully*) Marie-Céleste! … Hallo! Marie-Céleste! M … Hallo! (*He listens*)

There is no reply

There's no-one here. There's no-one about — and yet … Marie-Céleste! … Look, here's a table all set for breakfast … (*He touches the coffee pot*) Ow! … Hot coffee — and croissants — and English toast — and marmalade — such luxuries — but no-one here. Marie-Céleste! … Are you here? Hallo! … No reply … Well, I'll wait — I'll sit down and wait. (*He sits at the table*) And I'll have a slice of English toast and some marmalade. (*He spreads the toast with marmalade during the following*) The truth is I'm famished … You can't just wait around outside an apartment all night without feeling a few hunger pangs … I was just about to give it all up and go home when dawn broke and I was able to slip in as the old concierge slipped out … All that waiting

— but it will have been worthwhile if I can just see her, talk to her ... Such a ravishing beauty — Marie-Céleste! (*He makes to take a bite*)

Honorine, the maid, enters with a feather duster

Marcel stands

Honorine How dare you make yourself at home like that. Put down that toast this minute.

Marcel But I've just spread it with marmalade.

Honorine It is of no consequence to me with what you have spread it — put it down. You are not here to eat breakfast.

Marcel (*putting the slice of toast on a chair*) You are right! You are so very right.

Honorine (*aside, to the audience*) Really, tradesmen do take far too many liberties these days — I blame the Revolution. (*To Marcel*) And are you fully equipped?

Marcel Equipped?

Honorine Or do you have a minion or assistant who does all that sort of thing?

Marcel Assistant? (*He looks about himself*)

Honorine (*aside, to the audience*) It's obviously too early in the morning for him. (*To Marcel*) Never mind. Come through and I'll show you where to go. Madame has been waiting for weeks.

Marcel Ah ... Madame! ... Ah, yes! Yes, indeed, madame. That's who I've come to see ... That's who I'm longing to see — dying to see ...

Honorine   (*aside; to the audience*) Who would expect such dedication from a chimney sweep? (*To Marcel*) I think madame might well say the same about you, monsieur.

Marcel You think so? You really think she might? About — me?

Honorine I'm sure of it. Why, your name has been on her lips constantly.

Marcel (*to the audience*) And I never realized she even knew my name. (*To Honorine*) Tell me, does she speak of me — fondly?

Honorine I don't know about "fondly", but she's frequently said "When the devil is he going to come round?" Does that count?

Marcel Oh it does to me! It does to me! (*Aside*) Such comments hide the fervour — the true passion — I feel sure.

Honorine Look — you go and get whatever you need — but don't touch the breakfast ... I'll go and put the sheets out ready for you ...

Honorine exits R

Marcel Sheets? Put the sheets out? Good heavens, she really must be eager for me — as I am for her. This is how actresses behave — it must be ... Ever since I saw her dancing at *Le Lapin Méchant* I have known she must be mine. This isn't the first time I have followed her home — oh no, dear me, no — but this time will be different — and she will know how much I admire, adore — love her. I will embrace her — hold her to me — I don't know how many times — and ——

Honorine enters R

Honorine Will two do? Or will you need more?
Marcel What? More?
Honorine I'll put out three ... Better to be safe than sorry.

Honorine exits R

Marcel So direct. So outspoken. I have read about the maids of actresses — in novels; they look after their mistresses in this way — pandering to their every whim — to their gentlemen friends ... This is all new to me, but I mustn't let on ... I must drink it all in, savour it to the full.

Honorine enters

Honorine Done! Done! The room is prepared for you. (*Pause*) Well? ... Are you ready?

Marcel And keen — eager ... I've done this before you know.
Honorine I should hope you have, monsieur.
Marcel Your mistress will not be disappointed. Oh if only you knew how much I have looked forward to this moment.
Honorine Your dedication amazes me, monsieur.
Marcel Shall I go through? (*He moves to exit* R)
Honorine But, monsieur — surely not like that ...?

Marcel gives Honorine a querulous look

You are hardly — dressed for the job — are you?
Marcel (*to the audience*) They know so much. (*To Honorine*) You are right. I must — prepare myself.
Honorine I thought you would have done it by now ... Look, I'll go and move the furniture back to give you space ... Don't be too long, will you? Madame wants the job doing quickly.

Honorine exits R

Marcel Does she now? Quickly, eh? Well, we'll just have to see about — that — my little vixen ... (*He moves to the screen*)

Honorine enters R

Honorine You don't make too much of a mess do you?
Marcel What?
Honorine You'd better not.

Honorine exits R

Marcel (*to the audience*) So forthright. Such personal questions. I'll just go behind here (*the screen*) and — get ready. Oh ho! Marcel Morisot — this is undoubtedly your lucky day.

Marcel goes behind the screen and removes his jacket, waistcoat, shirt, trousers and possibly shoes too; they are all flung over the screen so that the audience is in no doubt about what he is doing. He sings "La Marseillaise" as he disrobes

Marcel (*singing*) Allons, enfants de la Patrie
                          Le jour de gloire est arrivé
                          Contre nous de la tyrannie … la la la
                          Dum dum la la la!
                          La la la la dum dum la la
                          La la la la …
                          Aux armes citoyons!
                          Formez — vos bataillons!
                          Marchons! Marchons! La la la la
                          La la la la la la!

Honorine enters brandishing an outrageous flue-brush

Honorine Will you need one of these?
Marcel (*peering out from one end of the screen*) I most certainly
    hope not!
Honorine Well the last one did — said he needed it to start things
    off with …

Honorine exits

*Marcel looks at the audience, dumbfounded, then disappears
behind the screen*

Yvette, Madame Signac, enters from L. She peers in a little warily

Yvette (*calling off*) Come along now — you've nothing to be afraid
    of … You are welcome here — come along.
Marcel Right!
Yvette What was that? (*She moves round the screen from the L end*)

*Marcel comes round the R end of the screen and, seeing Yvette
disappear behind the screen, moves across to follow her*

Marcel It's that decrepit old concierge, what on earth is she doing
    in this apartment? (*He goes behind the the L end of the screen*)

Yvette (*re-appearing at the* R *end of the screen*) No-one there — and yet I could have sworn … (*She sees the clothes and collects them up during the following*) Oh good heavens! What has Vincent been up to? How many times has a wife to tell her husband to put his clothes away, and not just leave them lying about anywhere? Will he never learn?

Yvette sweeps off R

(*Off*) Honorine! Honorine! Where is that girl? Honorine!

Claude Vallette, a filthy old tramp, staggers on L. *He carries a bottle and is a little worse for drink*

Claude Sorry … Sorry — to keep you — waiting … I was just — you see I've never — never … My word — this is … this is … this really is … I must be — dreaming. (*He drinks from his bottle*) What am I doing in …? What …? Who am I?… Where is this … ? What? … I need a drink … (*He drinks again and sits down on the marmaladed toast*) Aargh, that's better … Oops — what's this? … What is …? What …? (*He retrieves the toast*) It's … It's … What is it …? (*He tastes it*) It's marma… Marma …

Honorine enters

Honorine Don't do that … How many times …? (*She slaps his hand*) Well, at least you look the part now … What's that smell?
Claude Marmalade … I remember …

Honorine shows Claude out R *during the following*

Honorine Oh, come on, get the job done, madame will be back shortly … It's straight through there.
Claude Is it? … Through … Through … Is it? … Right.

Claude blunders off R. *We hear him off stage*

(*Off*) Aha! Ha!

Honorine Is that what he means by getting ready — drinking? Who would have thought that such a mundane task needed dutch courage.

Marcel Psst! Psst!

Honorine There's no other word for it. What was that?

Yvette enters R. *She wears a cloak*

Yvette Psst! Psst! Honorine! There you are ... I've put my husband's clothes in his dressing-room, do try to ensure that he puts them away in future. (*To the audience*) Though heaven knows why he takes them off in the hall anyway.

Honorine Yes, madame.

Yvette Take my cloak.

Honorine takes Yvette's cloak

Now where is our guest of the day?

Marcel's hand waves above the screen. Honorine shrugs

Yvette Dear Honorine, you're such a naïve little thing. You can't get used to the idea, can you? When you are as successful and affluent as we are, you will realize it behoves us to help the less fortunate. That's why every morning I go out early on to the streets of Paris — and bring back some poor unfortunate for breakfast ... It's my piece of charity ... Now where is this morning's fortunate unfortunate?

Honorine I haven't seen him.

Yvette I left him here ... He can't have gone far ... He seemed to have difficulty in walking, poor fellow ...

Honorine Don't they all?

Yvette Don't just stand there, Honorine, look for the poor fellow ... He'll be bewildered — and confused ...

Honorine (*aside*) I share those feelings. (*She puts the cloak down and looks around*)

Yvette I'll just see if he has crept out into the street again.

Yvette exits L

During the following speech, Marcel creeps out and stands behind Honorine, bewildered

Honorine Every morning it's the same: make a breakfast for our "guest" … Every morning she's out like a lark dragging some "poor unfortunate" back with her. The family silver is disappearing at a huge rate of knots … Still, I suppose she means well … Now where can he have got to?

Marcel (*touching Honorine's shoulder*) Excuse me!

Honorine Aargh! There you are! No — you're not … My word, you've been quick … Is it done?

Marcel What? (*Meaning "pardon"*)

Honorine Clean. Is it clean? Where are your old clothes?

Marcel What do you mean, old …?

Honorine Have it your way … Where are they?

Marcel The concierge took them — said her husband had left them here.

Honorine The concierge isn't married.

Yvette (*off*) Any success, Honorine?

Honorine I'm not sure.

Yvette (*off*) What do you mean by that? "Not sure" … Honorine?

Marcel She mustn't see me like this.

Honorine (*giving Marcel Yvette's cloak*) Put this on and sit down, keep your head down.

Marcel puts the cloak on, puts the hood up and sits at the table

Yvette enters

Either he's here — or he's not … Ah … Yes — so you did find him then? (*To Marcel*) Naughty boy, running off from your benefactress like that. (*Aside, to Honorine*) Why is he wearing my cloak, Honorine?

Honorine Cold. He said he was cold. Shivering … He was cold and shivering.
Yvette Poor soul … Eat, monsieur, eat; it will help you.

Marcel eats

Really, Honorine, the more desperate they are, the more my heart goes out to them. If only my husband would recognize the value of the work I do in this way.
Honorine Your husband doesn't understand you, madame.
Yvette Ah … (*Aside*) Out of the mouths of babes and sucklings, you know, Honorine, only last night my Vincent said to me that if he caught one more of my — unfortunates — in the house he would shoot him like a dog.

Marcel chokes

Are you all right, monsieur?

Marcel coughs more

Could it be pneumonia, Honorine? I don't like the look of him.
Honorine (*aside*) I'm beginning to hate the sight of him
Yvette (*to Marcel*) Drink some coffee … It will warm you through.

There are a crash and a yell off R

What was that, Honorine?
Honorine I don't like to think.
Yvette Are you entertaining someone in your room, Honorine?
Claude (*off, singing from "The Merry Widow"*) You'll find me at Maxim's, where everyone — has — la la la la la (*etc.*). I say — just look at this, eh?
Yvette Honorine … Who is that — voice?
Honorine The chimney sweep's assistant?
Yvette The sweep?
Honorine For the chimneys. He arrived just after you had left on your errand of mercy.

Yvette Yes, now I think about it there was an unsavoury character
    lurking at our door.
Marcel I wasn't lurking — I've never lurked in my life.
Yvette Not you, monsieur. Enjoy your breakfast. (*To Honorine*)
    You see how guilt-ridden the downtrodden are? Yet another
    reason for us to be merciful.

There is another crash off stage

Claude   (*off*) Whoops! Butter-fniggers! No — fingers —
    fingerbuttons ...
Yvette   Is he capable, Honorine? Does he know what he is doing
    in there? Go and see what he's doing now and tell him to stop it,
    and to come here at once.

Honorine heads for the exit R

    Yes, madame ... If you insist. (*Aside*) There's never a moment's
    peace in this house.

Honorine exits

Yvette (*to Marcel*) Now tell me — how did you come to this parlous
    condition? What was your family like? Were you one of many?
    Tell me about the oppression — share it with me.

Marcel offers Yvette a croissant

    No — no — no ... Your deprivation — let it all pour out — let
    it pour out ——

Marcel pours Yvette some coffee

    — and I want to understand your squalor ... I need to know of your
    hardship ...

A door slams off L. *Monsieur Vincent Signac is home!*

Signac (*off*) Damn and blast! Will I never learn? Honorine! Honorine ̄
   Where is the dratted girl? Never around when she's wanted ̄
   Honorine!
Yvette It's my husband. Is that you, Vincent?
Signac (*off*) No, *it's not!* Who do you think it is, you dimwittec ̄
   individual? Why did I have to marry the least intelligent woman ̄
   in the whole of the Western World?
Yvette Well, it sounds like you.

Honorine enters R

Honorine Madame, it's monsieur.
Signac (*off*) Honorine! Here! At once!
Yvette I believe you're right.
Honorine I must go and see what he wants …

There is a crash of crockery off stage R *and hysterical laughter from*
Claude

Signac (*off*) Honorine! Come and help me with these documents!
Honorine Coming, monsieur.
Signac (*off*) Honorine! How many more times? I need you. I've got
   to find my shotgun.
Yvette Shotgun?
Honorine I'm on my way, monsieur.

Honorine exits L

Yvette Shotgun! (*To Marcel*) Shotgun, monsieur!

Marcel gives a strangled cry

Yvette Quick — behind the screen — there's no time to waste. If
   my husband sees you — you are dead as a dado.
Marcel Dodo! (*He hides behind the screen*)
Yvette That's the one.

There is a crash of crockery from off stage

Claude (*off*) Oops, there goes another one.

Yvette takes Marcel's place at the breakfast table

Signac enters L *in a rage, followed by Honorine carrying vast quantities of documents and books, and a briefcase*

Signac Damnation! Utter damnation! You can never find anything in this house when you need it.
Yvette If you put things away properly then you'd know where they were.
Signac (*to the audience*) Why does one's wife always sound like one's mother on occasions like this?
Yvette If it's your clothes, I know where you left them.
Signac Clothes? What d'you mean clothes? It's the shotgun I'm talking about.
Yvette And why might you want that, dear?
Signac Because I'm going to play golf — what do you think I want a shotgun for?
Yvette You're not a member of a golf club, dear.
Signac I'm married to a lunatic — I'm going to shoot myself, aren't I?
Yvette Then you'll definitely need a gun, dear.
Honorine Monsieur doesn't mean it, madame. It's just his jest.
Signac Keep your servant's nose out of my business — I'll shoot myself if I like — and if I can find the damned gun — why isn't it near the front door with the umbrellas?
Yvette Perhaps someone took it by mistake, Vincent — thinking it was an umbrella.
Signac (*to the audience*) Her mother went the same way — the brain turned to blancmange and she had to be locked away.
Yvette We've had some very inclement weather recently — quite heavy showers ...
Signac Will you stop this! Stop! Stop! And listen ... I have been out at a client's — an old client's — a revered client, or so I thought

—and I've just returned with an armful of documents—show her Honorine—all of which inform me that I must find four million francs *toute de suite* or there is no solution but for me to shoot myself.

Yvette So that's why you want the gun, is it, dear?

Signac Unless you've got four million francs.

Honorine Perhaps there's been some mistake, monsieur?

Signac Mistake? I'm a lawyer, damnit, my client is another lawyer — we don't make mistakes, except when we're dealing with the public. What am I going to do?

Yvette You'll have to buy another one.

Signac (*to Honorine*) What is she talking about?

Yvette Another gun — if you've lost the one you had!

Honorine Madame is only trying to be helpful, monsieur.

Signac Oh yes — stick together — stand up for each other ... Women! They're as inseparable as — as — as — coathangers when the going gets difficult.

Yvette When did you last use it, Vincent? The gun?

Signac How should I know?

Yvette You might remember where it is, if you can remember when you last used it ... Do you want coffee? Get another cup, Honorine.

Honorine Yes, madame. (*She makes to go, still holding all the documents*)

Signac Don't take those with you, you silly girl, I need to work on them ... Leave them here.

Honorine just drops the documents, books and briefcase, and exits R

I said "leave" them not abandon them. Oh, great heavens, now they'll be in no order at all. Let me see ... (*He shuffles through the documents*) There must be some way out of this mess.

Yvette Are you working, dear?

Signac No, I'm taking the dog for a walk! Of course I'm working — I'm always working.

Yvette Perhaps I can help ... What are we looking for?

Signac Stop! Don't touch anything, Yvette ... You keep on saving
your tramps, and let me deal with real work ...

Yvette They are not tramps, Vincent — they are some of the
world's unfortunates.

Signac Well, we'll be joining them very shortly — if I can't find
this money or the solution to my legal problem.

Yvette Oh it's a *legal* problem is it? You need a lawyer.

Signac I *am* a lawyer! Damnit!

Honorine screams, off, then enters R

Honorine Madame! Madame! Monsieur!

Signac What now?

Honorine In there — out there ... He's — he's ... he's rifling your
drawers.

Signac (*to Yvette*) Is this one of your down-and-outs?

Yvette Not at all! My tramp for today is behind the screen.

Signac What? *What?* He's where? Honorine — fetch me my
shotgun!

Honorine Yes, sir — where is it?

Signac Don't make difficulties — go and — get — it.

Honorine (*moving* L) Yes, sir! Certainly, sir! (*To the audience*) If
he doesn't know where it is, how am I expected to know.

Honorine exits L

Signac (*to the audience*) Other men's wives collect lovers, mine
prefers derelicts.

Yvette (*to the audience*) I so admire my husband when he's being
positive — but I don't let him know it. (*To Signac*) Oh, Vincent
— don't do it, don't do it — show some human kindness. (*She
grabs Signac*)

Signac Unhand me, woman — a man's got to do what a man's got
to do ... Honorine!

Honorine enters L *carrying an umbrella. She gives a shrug to the
audience*

Honorine Sir?
Signac (*still looking at Yvette*) Give it to me!

Honorine looks at the umbrella

Signac Quickly, girl! Give it me!

Honorine hands Signac the umbrella. He handles it like a shotgun

> Stand back the pair of you. Now then! You — behind the screen
> — come out where I can see you — and don't try anything funny
> — do you hear … ?

Marcel emerges, his eyes closed

Marcel Don't shoot me, sir! I daren't look. Please don't shoot me
… Oh, I really daren't look … Have mercy — I beg you …
Signac Stand there … Don't you move a step further — or I'll shoot
you like a … (*he realizes he has an umbrella in his hand*) like a
— like a … (*he looks at Honorine*)

Honorine shrugs

> … like … (*He looks to Yvette*)
Yvette Cats and dogs?

Signac opens his umbrella and holds it above himself

Marcel Sir! Sir! Let me explain … (*He opens his eyes*) Where are
you? Ah, there! … Sir! Sir! Please, I implore you — don't shoot!
Please don't shoot! I'm not what you think I am … (*He takes in
the situation*) I'm … I'm … (*He holds out his hand to see if it's
raining*) Where's your gun?
Signac Precisely.
Marcel What?

Signac Do you know anything about it? Was it you?

Yvette You don't need it now, Vincent.

Honorine Not now you've got your umbrella.

Signac Don't be facetious, Honorine, it doesn't suit you ——

Honorine Yes, sir.

Signac (*giving Honorine the umbrella*) — and hold that. (*To Marcel*) When did you see it last?

Marcel What? What last?

Signac The gun! My gun! Don't prevaricate — I might become physical.

Yvette No! Vincent! Not that! Oh, tell him where his gun is.

Marcel How should I know?

Signac Don't lie to me — you tramps are all the same. You lie like cheap stair-carpet ——

Marcel But I'm not a tramp.

Signac You see, proof positive — the damn fellow's at it all the time.

Yvette A deprived childhood, Vincent ... we must make allowances ...

Marcel I'm *not* a tramp! I'm *not*! I'm *not*!

Honorine It's true, sir, he's not a tramp — he's a chimney sweep.

Signac What?

Marcel What?!!

Yvette So why's he wearing my cloak — and he ate breakfast like a tramp.

Signac A chimney sweep?

Marcel Sweep?

Honorine Come to brush out our flues.

Signac Eh?

Yvette You despicable man! You misled me! Masquerading as an unfortunate when all the time you were sweeping chimneys.

Marcel I deny it! I've never swept a chimney in my life.

Yvette (*snatching away the cloak Marcel is wearing*) Give me back my cloak this instant and it'll cost you five francs for the breakfast.

Marcel Five francs? (*He realizes he is now in his underwear*) Ooh!

Yvette (*seeing the underwear*) Oh, heavens!

Signac Too cheap! Yvette, we'll never make money if you only charge such paltry amounts ... Wait a minute (*to Marcel*) where are your clothes?Just what do you think you're doing in your underwear? (*Accusingly*) Yvette!

Yvette Nothing to do with me, dear — he's not one of mine.

Signac (*to Honorine; accusingly*) Honorine?

Honorine He told me he was the chimney sweep.

Marcel I never did!

Honorine And he took his clothes off ready for work, didn't you?

Marcel Well yes, but ——

Signac But what? What work were you going to do then — in your underwear?

Marcel Er ... er ... (*He shrugs to the audience*)

Signac Come on man, what explanation have you?

Marcel Explanation? Ah — listen ...

Claude (*off*) My God — look at all this — this ... I say! Must be worth a fortune — a fortune — aha! Ha! Ha! (*He laughs*)

Signac What the hell's that?

Honorine It's the chimney sweep's assistant.

Signac Do you mean there's two of these devils? Don't just stand there, Honorine — fetch me my shotgun — I'll need both barrels.

Marcel Oh sir! You're not going to shoot me are you?

Signac Of course not — I'm going to shoot both of you ... Get the gun, Honorine — don't just stand there ...

Yvette I thought you'd misplaced it, Vincent.

Signac Misplaced? Great heavens, woman, what sort of an incompetent do you think I am? It's in the wardrobe — go and get it, Honorine.

Honorine In the wardrobe?

Signac Where else?

Honorine heads for the exit R

Honorine (*handing the umbrella to Marcel* en route) Hold this! (*She pauses and turns*) Your shotgun, sir?

Signac In the wardrobe — you can't miss it!

Claude (*off; very big*) *Aha! Aha!* Bang! Bang! Hands up your sticks, eh? ... Ha! Ha! Bang! Bang!

Those on stage realize what has happened off

Honorine (*stage whisper*) I think — it's too late — sir!
Yvette (*stage whisper*) Why on earth did you put it in the wardrobe, Vincent?
Marcel (*stage whisper; to the audience*) I shall never go to the theatre again.

Yvette, Marcel and Honorine huddle together under the umbrella

Signac (*shouting*) You just put that gun down, sir — and that's an order! Do you hear me?
Claude (*off; calling back*) And you just put your hands up, sir, or I shall come in there and — and — and be with you! Ha! Ha! Bang! Bang!
Signac I'm in no humour to bandy words with you — put the gun down — now. Or have I to come and get it?
Yvette Vincent! No! ... He may be armed.
Signac He is armed you stupid woman — that's the whole point. I shall count to five then I'm coming for you.
Claude (*off*) O-ho!
Signac One — two ... Did you hear me?
Claude (*off*) Buckle my shoe!
Signac Right! That's it! You confounded nuisance ...

Signac stalks off R, *only to return almost immediately, backwards followed by Claude, pointing the shotgun at his chest. Claude carries also a sheet or similar in which his loot is being carried, and wears a flamboyant dancer's headdress, earrings, necklaces and bracelets, all diamanté*

Claude Three — four — knock at the ...
Yvette Door.
Signac Don't encourage him, Yvette! And put that gun down — sir — I will not tell you again.
Claude Now then — what have we here? Eh?
Signac Did you hear me?

Claude Put up your hands and give me your watch and your wallet.
Signac What?
Claude Watch where you put your hands and up with your wallet.
Signac The man's demented — I shall have him arrested.
Yvette Be careful, Vincent — he has a gun — and he's wearing my
    jewellery.
Claude Bang! Bang! Ha! Ha! Hands up — this is a hold stick …
Honorine He means a hold-up, sir.
Claude That's it! You've got it … Hands up and give me your
    wallet.

Signac puts his hands up

    Come on.
Signac I can't give you my wallet if my hands are up.
Yvette I'll get it for him shall I, Vincent? (*She makes to do so*)
Signac You'll do no such thing …
Claude And your watch — quickly.
Yvette I think you should do as he asks, Vincent — he looks quite
    determined …
Honorine (*to Marcel*) Can't you control your assistant …
Marcel I haven't got an assistant …
Claude Now it's my turn to count — up — to … *up* — to …
Yvette Five?
Signac Don't make it any easier for him, Yvette.
Claude How many?
Honorine A hundred.
Claude Right — a hundred, right … one — two —— (*He carries*
    on counting during the following and puts his bundle down)
Signac What did you do that for?
Claude — five — six — seven —— (*etc.*)
Marcel I feel sick.
Honorine Perhaps it was the breakfast — something you ate.
Claude — nine — ten … (*etc.*)
Yvette Poor fellow … He lacks a proper education.
Signac So is this one of yours then, Yvette?
Yvette They are denied so much.

Signac I can't stand here with my hands up all day …
Honorine Put them down, sir, he's still busy counting.
Marcel I feel sick … I need a drink.
Honorine Are you thirsty?
Claude Thirsty-one, thirsty-two, thirsty-three … (*etc.*)
Signac Don't give him anything, Honorine—he hasn't paid for his breakfast yet.
Marcel But I haven't any money — it was in my jacket.
Yvette So you *are* destitute …
Marcel At the moment …
Yvette Well, I'll have *you* instead … Were you ill-treated at home — abused, perhaps?
Signac Stop that, Yvette … He's not an unfortunate, he's a … What did you say he was, Honorine … ?
Honorine A sweep. He's a sweep. '
Signac He looks wide awake to me …
Honorine No, sir, a chimney sweep and (*she indicates Claude*) — he's one too.
Claude Three — four — five —— (*etc.*)
Yvette These poor follows have to take on such mundane tasks to eke out an existence.
Marcel I am *not* a chimney sweep. How many times must I reiterate this. I am *not*. And I do not have an assistant — and if I did it certainly wouldn't be *him*.
Honorine So what are you doing here then?
Yvette Precisely — under false pretences?
Signac And under my umbrella!
Marcel (*to the audience*) There's nothing else for it, I shall have to tell the truth. (*To the onstage trio of Yvette, Honorine and Signac*) Let me tell you the truth … (*He dramatically closes the umbrella and gives it to Honorine*) I am a lover of the theatre …
Yvette I knew he was an unfortunate.
Signac Quiet, Yvette …
Marcel More that that I am a lover of cabaret — and particularly a lover of the *Le Lapin Méchant*, and the dancers there — and one of them above all others.
Signac How many are there?

Honorine Fifteen! (*Then she wishes she hadn't spoken*)

Claude Sixteen — seventeen — eighteen ——(*etc.*)

Signac So many?

Marcel But, sir ... Ah, but — sir ... This one is far above all others, she is perfection ... She moves with elegance, with style — with true panache, with grace — and she has — captured — my heart ... I adore her ...

Signac I should stick to being a chimney sweep ... She'll only bring you trouble — it's woman's chief purpose in life.

Yvette Oh, Vincent — how could you?

Marcel So, last night, after the show — I waited — and I followed the love of my life home — to her apartment — where I hoped I could press my suit.

Yvette So it was yours was it — I thought it was Vincent's, he's always leaving his things lying about. (*She indicates the papers on the floor*) Just look at all this lot.

Marcel I waited all night — till chance favoured me and I was able to sneak into her apartment ——

Signac So what are you doing here then?

Marcel — to seek my Marie-Céleste.

Signac There's no dancer here. Unless — Yvette, you haven't taken up terpsichore have you?

Yvette I hardly ever drink, you know that.

Signac No dancers here, young man; you took off your clothes in vain. My wife hasn't danced in earnest since she was twenty.

Claude Twenty-one, twenty-two — twenty-three —— (*etc.*)

Marcel But I saw her — I followed her — I saw her enter *this* apartment ...

All but Claude turn to look questioningly at Honorine

Honorine does a little dance with the umbrella, singing to the tune of "You'll Find Me at Maxim's"

Honorine (*singing*) I'm called Marie-Céleste
                I really am the best
                For when they see me dancing

    The men find I'm entrancing
    The other girls you know
    Have not got much to show
    So all the patrons call for, La Belle
    Marie-Céleste! (*She strikes a suitable pose*)

Signac Do you know this woman, Honorine?

Marcel Marie-Céleste — is it you?

Honorine twirls seductively, and she and Marcel embrace

Yvette Honorine, unhand my vagrant!

Signac What is going on here, Yvette? (*To the audience*) Really, I don't think I'll ever understand women if I live to be ninety.

Claude Ninety-one, ninety-two, ninety-three —— (*etc.*)

Honorine Let me go and find your trousers …

Marcel Let me take you away from all this …

Yvette (*to Marcel*) Let me help you find a proper life — not out on the streets any more …

Signac Let me understand this … All is not what it seemed — am I right?

Claude One hundred! Coming — ready or not … Now — where's everyone hiding? Eh? Just let me see … (*He gives the gun to Signac*) Hold this … Now, where can you be?

Claude blunders round the stage, looking for people. He sees the screen and moves behind it

Aha! Anybody behind there? … Just let me have a lootle lick.

Signac What's he up to now? Damn fellow.

Marcel (*to Honorine, fondly*) Marie-Céleste — or do I mean Honorine?

Honorine And who are you? My — what?

Marcel Marcel. Will you marry me?

Yvette (*looking at Claude's bundle*) Look at this, Vincent … All our best silver — jewellery — knick-knacks … I do believe he was stealing them.

Signac I do believe you may be right ... When he comes out from behind the screen I'll blow his head off.

Yvette How despicable! What a thing to do! After I was so kind and considerate ... I'll never rescue another unfortunate again — not as long as I live.

Signac I'm so pleased to hear it, my dear.

Honorine Monsieur — madame — I must reluctantly tender my resignation from your employ.

Signac Your mother's not sick again, I trust, Honorine.

Honorine No, sir — I have just agreed to marry this gentleman.

Signac A chimney sweep — what d'you want to marry a chimney sweep for?

Marcel I'm not a sweep — I really am not a sweep.

Signac I could've sworn someone told me you were.

Yvette He was one of my unfortunates, Vincent.

Marcel would correct her, but Honorine prevents his so doing

Signac So now I am your only unfortunate, Yvette. (*He sits among the papers*)

Yvette What do you mean, Vincent?

Signac Ye gods, woman, don't you ever listen? Didn't I say: the case — the papers — the contested will — four million francs that I have to pay because I failed to find this beneficiary ... I've searched — all these documents — the national registry ... All my legal training and background has failed me. I needed to find this — this — miserable individual — this one man — by today — or forfeit four million francs. And I have failed ... I haven't discovered him ... He could be anywhere — this Marcel Morisot — cretin.

Marcel Wait! What was that you called him?

Signac A cretin — it's a legal term ...

Marcel But — monsieur — I am Marcel Morisot.

Signac (*picking up a paper*) Marcel Morisot, son of Pierre and Louise Morisot of Alsace ——

Marcel That's me ...

Signac (*another paper*) — whose family business of Morisot and Furneaux flourished in Avignon in the beginning of (*another paper*) this century (*another paper*) and whose only brothers and sisters were tragically killed in the eruption on Martinique ——

Marcel I am he!

Signac (*another paper*) — and who has a most vivid and unusual birthmark on his left (*another paper*) — buttock.

Honorine (*with a look down Marcel's underwear*) Yes! Yes! Oh yes!

Signac Saved! I'm saved! Saved! Oh, Yvette, we can hold up our heads once more in society. I am cleared — I am exonerated ... We have no more cares in the world. (*He embraces Yvette*)

Marcel And I have found my Marie-Céleste.

Honorine And I my own Marcel.

They embrace too. Claude comes out from behind the screen

Claude Nobody there ... So where can they ... (*He sees the others*) Aha! You're caught — all of you ... Now it's *my* turn. Don't forget to — count.

Music plays. Claude dances to it, remarkably competently

I'm going — now — to hide — (*he dances towards the wings*) and if you can't find me — I'll be in the bar next door.

Claude exits L

CURTAIN

FURNITURE AND PROPERTY LIST

On stage: Dining-room furniture
On table: breakfast for one including coffee; toast and marmalade; croissants
Screen

Off stage: Feather duster (**Honorine**)
Outrageous flue-brush (**Honorine**)
Bottle (**Claude**)
Vast quantities of documents and books; briefcase (**Honorine**)
Umbrella (**Honorine**)
Shotgun (**Claude**)*
Sheet full of "loot" (**Claude**)

* See p. 28 for a note about the Firearms (Amendment) Bill

LIGHTING PLOT

Practical fittings required: nil.
Interior. The same throughout.

To open: General interior lighting

No cues

EFFECTS PLOT

Cue 1	**Yvette**: "It will warm you through." *Crash*	(Page 9)
Cue 2	**Yvette**: " … for us to be merciful." *Crash*	(Page 10)
Cue 3	**Yvette**: " … to know of your hardship …" *Door slam*	(Page 10)
Cue 4	**Honorine**: "I must go and see what he wants …" *Crash of crockery*	(Page 11)
Cue 5	**Yvette**: "That's the one." *Crash of crockery*	(Page 11)
Cue 6	**Claude**: "Don't forget to — count." *Music*	(Page 24)

THE FIREARMS (AMENDMENT) BILL

Samuel French is grateful to Charles Vance, Vice-Chairman of the Theatres Advisory Council, for the following information regarding the Firearms (Amendment) Bill:

"The Firearms (Amendment) Bill does not affect blank-firing pistols which are not readily convertible (i.e. those which do not require a Firearms Certificate). Among the reasons against imposing restrictions on such items is their use in theatre, cinema and television as a 'safe' alternative to real guns.

The general prohibition on the possession of real handguns will apply to those used for theatrical purposes. It would clearly be anomalous to prohibit the use of those items for target shooting, but permit their use for purposes where a fully-working gun is not needed. As handguns will become 'Section 5' prohibited weapons, they would fall under the same arrangements as at present apply to real machine guns. As you will know, there are companies which are authorized by the Secretary of State to supply such weapons for theatrical purposes.

The exemption under Section 12 of the Firearms Act 1968, whereby actors can use firearms without themselves having a Firearms Certificate, will remain in force."

Regulations apply to the United Kingdom only. Producers in other countries should refer to appropriate legislation.